THE TRADITIONAL DEFINITION OF YOUTH IN BODO SOCIETY AND THE VIOLATION OF THE RIGHT TO PRIVACY IN MARITAL STATUS IN THE AGE OF GLOBALISATION

STUDY SUBMITTED TO PRESENT ORALLY AT 8TH INTERNATIONAL "BASKENT" CONGRESS ON HUMANITIES AND SOCIAL SCIENCES ON FEBRUARY 04-06, 2023

RITURAJ BASUMATARY

Contents

The traditional definition of Youth in Bodo Society and the violation of the Right to Privacy in marital status in the age of Globalisation

STUDY SUBMITTED TO PRESENT ORALLY AT 8TH INTERNATIONAL "BASKENT"CONGRESS ON HUMANITIES
AND SOCIAL SCIENCES ON FEBRUARY 04-06, 2023

Rituraj Basumatary
M.A., NET, SLET
MPHIL
Assistant Professor
Department of Political Science
Borobazar College

28.01.2023

Dear Rituraj BASUMATARY;

We are delighted to announce that your **"THE TRADITIONAL DEFINITION OF YOUTH IN BODO SOCIETY AND THE VIOLATION OF THE RIGHT TO PRIVACY IN MARITAL STATUS IN THE AGE OF GLOBALISATION"** study, which you submitted to present orally at 8th International "Başkent" Congress on Humanities and Social Sciences on February 04-06, 2023 has been accepted.

The paper you will present orally at our congress will be published in the proceedings book of our congress on February 13, 2023.

If you would like your full paper to be published in the congress proceedings book, please send it by e-mail until February 06, 2023.

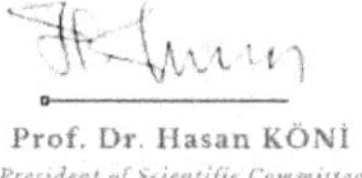

Prof. Dr. Hasan KÖNİ
President of Scientific Committee

Prof. Dr. Revan D. MAN
President of Organization Committee

CERTIFICATE

OF PARTICIPATION

THIS CERTIFICATE IS PROUDLY PRESENTED TO :

Rituraj BASUMATARY

participated in the 8TH INTERNATIONAL "BAŞKENT" CONGRESS ON HUMANITIES AND SOCIAL SCIENCES
on February 04-06, 2023 and orally presented the paper entitled
**"THE TRADITIONAL DEFINITION OF YOUTH IN BODO SOCIETY AND THE VIOLATION OF THE RIGHT TO PRIVACY
IN MARITAL STATUS IN THE AGE OF GLOBALISATION"**

Spc. Leyla ADANMIŞ
Organization Committee Member

Prof. Dr. Revan D. MAN
President of Organization Committee

Given this on February 04-06, 2023 at Ankara, Turkey.

I
Introduction

Youth generally means a young person. It is a common gender which consists of man, women and the other gender as well. There is no universally accepted definition of youth. But anyways it is measured with the help of age though the age ranges varies from each other.

II

Traditional definition of youth in Bodo Society

In traditional Bodo Society, youth is defined in a very unique way. It is measured with the help of marital status. In Bodo Society, a person is considered to be youth until and unless he is married. But if a person gets married, he is no longer going to be considered as an youth irrespective of his age.

III

Violation of the Right to Privacy in marital status

Youth is a very important part of our life. The number of youth population is also very important for a society. In most of the societies, youth is measured with the help of age even though the age ranges varies from one society to another. But in Bodo Society, if we wanted to find out the youth population, we are compelled to ask a person's marital status according to the traditional definition.

But now-a-days, the modern democratic laws does not permit it since it violates the Right to Privacy. In modern society, we have the right to keep our marital status private.

Some people criticise the traditional definition of youth in Bodo Society as a social evil. It is also in contradictory to modern laws.

But now-a-days, in this age of Globalisation, some changes also occurred in Bodo Society as we have seen that there are many married man, who are the leaders of youth organisation.

IV

Globalisation

Globalisation generally means Global Civilisation, which means the civilisation or the advancement of the globe. Globalisation has its impacts in different societies in different ways.
Just like other societies, we can find the impacts of Globalisation in Bodo Society too.

V

Conclusion

From the above discussion, we have come to know about the traditional definition of youth in Bodo Society. We have also come to know that it violates the Right to Privacy in marriage. But at the same time, we have also noticed that some changes have occurred in Bodo Society as a result of Globalisation. As we all know that Globalisation has its own merits and demerits as well as positive and negative impacts. Apart from its negative changes, Globalisation has brought some positive changes to some societies as well. So it is also our duty to let Globalisation be used for the well being of the people and the society.